SOMEBODY, PLEASE TELL ME THE TRUTH

"I am the way, the Truth, and the life: no man cometh to the Father but by me."
Jesus Christ

GAYNELL JONES MONTGOMERY

SOMEBODY, PLEASE TELL ME THE **TRUTH**

"I am the way, the Truth, and the life: no man cometh to the Father but by me."
Jesus Christ

GAYNELL JONES MONTGOMERY

Somebody, Please Tell Me The Truth

Copyright © 2016 by Gaynell Montgomery
P.O. Box 1112
Greeley, CO 80534

Published by Seaborough Enterprises Publishing, LLC
Savannah, GA

ISBN 9780984123568
Editorial Credits: Barbara Jones King
                   Fannie Jones Walker

Printed in the United States of America.

All rights reserved under International Copyright Law. Contents and/or cover may not be reproduced in whole or in part in any form without the express written consent of the Publisher.

All Scripture quotations are taken from the King James Version of the Bible.

The author's comments within Scripture quotations are enclosed in parentheses.

Table of Contents

Forward by:

Pastors Willie and Doris Miles

Pastor Wade A. Bell, Sr., D.D.

Mrs. Julia Jones

Forward	7
Dedication	11
Introduction	12
Truth Be Told	13
God Is The Playwright	18
Stop Telling Stories	25
Knowing Who You Are	31
God's Created Woman Of Virtue	36
God's Created Man Of Valor	45
Whose Helpmeet, Lord?	50

What's So Good About Grace?	60
Say Goodbye, Let Yesterday Die	68
So God, Why Am I This Color?	72
Don't Live Out the Blame Game!	77
His Truth Is Marching	81
We Hold These Truths	84
Prayer For Salvation	90
About the Author	91
For More Information	93

Forward

Pastors Willie and Dorris Miles, Sign of the Dove Church, Jackson, TN

We're so excited about what God is doing in the earth! Our sister, friend, and traveling evangelist, Gaynell, has allowed God to use her to "Tell the Truth." He has taught her fingers to fight! If you need salvation, deliverance, and/or healing, the pages of this book contain the truth of God's word that He wants you to know - which will make you free. The only thing that can free us in this hour is the Truth!

Pastor Wade A. Bell, Sr., D.D., Deeper Life Gospel Center, Redford, MI

We are combated with so many lies, now it is time for, "Somebody, Please Tell Me The Truth." The significance of this book for me is not only the credibility of the writer, but it's the pen of passion and persuasion in which she writes. Gaynell shares her experience of a spiritual awakening brought to her as a child that couldn't be shaken, ran from, or ignored. As you travel with her through the pages of her life, you will be amazed at times, captivated with suspense, and understand why the truth today is vitally a necessity and not an option. Having taught in the Christian community for the past 41 years, it is a delight to have been exposed to such a sound read.

Deception is one of the tools that causes something to appear one way, but really it's another. Lies that have been told to us about what we are, who we are, and what we cannot achieve have taken root and have caused many of us to detour from the path that God has for all of us.

If you are looking to be free from the destructive forces of deception - to the liberty, peace, joy, and prosperity of your God given life, then the truth in this literary work is what you need. Gaynell's timely book has arrived on the scene for you, and I hear your cry for, "Somebody, Please Tell Me The Truth."

Mrs. Julia Jones, My Mother and My First Evangelist, Greenville, MS

Having birthed fifteen (15) children, who, as of this writing, are all alive, in their right minds, and blessed immeasurably, I have lived and breathed Psalm 23 that declares:

1 The Lord is my shepherd; I shall not want.

2 He maketh me to lie down in green pastures: he leadeth me beside the still waters.

3 He restoreth my soul: he leadeth me in the paths of righteousness for his name's sake.

4 Yea, though I walk through the valley of the shadow of death, I will fear no evil: for thou art with me; thy rod and thy staff they comfort me.

5 Thou preparest a table before me in the presence of mine enemies: thou anointest my head with oil; my cup runneth over.

6 Surely goodness and mercy shall follow me all the days of my life: and I will dwell in the house of the Lord for ever.

The Lord is truly MY shepherd…and yours too, whether you know it or not, today and every day. All of my children were taught the things of God at an early age. They were only taught the teachings of the Holy Bible, and not strange doctrines and religions. I took God very seriously when He said in Proverbs 22:6, "Train up a child in the way he should go: and when he is old, he will not depart from it."

There is no other truth! I thank God for my daughter, and the gift He has given her; to share the truth with men, women, boys, and girls all over the world.

Dedication

Thank you Jesus for pouring this book into me – I am so privileged.

To my earthly daddy, the late Mr. Elbert Jones, Sr., who was truly an officer and a gentleman. Surely, it is written in the pages of glory that you were a hero to so many.

To my mama – Mrs. Julia Miriam Jones and my brothers and sisters – I love you. Thank you for your lives, your examples, and all of your love and support.

To my dear friends, Patrick and Dorothy Dotson, I love you and appreciate all that you have been during this journey. To all of my brothers and sisters in Christ, you have been simply the best encouragers that a woman of God could have!

A very special thanks to my Editors of Excellence – Mrs. Fannie Jones Walker and Mrs. Barbara Jones King. Thank you for your patience, tolerance, and so much more! You are such a blessing!

Introduction

Gaynell wants to share her personal experiences that will enlighten and broaden your worldview of things past, present, and that which is to come. "God has been and continues to be the real, guiding force in my life."

There are many thoughts, philosophies, religions, denominations, disciplines, and yes, even lies that permeate our everyday lives - our homes, jobs, schools, and relationships. Everyone in the world needs to understand and know that there is hope, healing, and help for them *RIGHT NOW*!

With consideration of unstable and unpredictable current world events, Gaynell declares that the Bible is the unadulterated and uncompromised Word of God and Truth for the whole world, *NOW*!

Truth Be Told

"Gaynell, wake up. Gaynell, you've gotta get up for church. Alright, when I come back, you had better be up." These were the words of my mother, who along with my father parented fifteen (15) children. They made sure that we went to church every Sunday. It was routine for my mother to wake all of us so we could get washed-up and dressed-up in order to go serve the Lord at His house. What my mother didn't know - was that at that very moment, I *couldn't* wake up. God was busy telling her little girl THE TRUTH.

"Where are we going? Where's my mother? Where's my brother? (My best friend and partner in crime – Elbert, Jr., or "Main" as he was affectionately called by the family). Why can't I see or hear any of my sisters or brothers? Help! Where are we going?" The next thing I knew, I was being led by two gigantic creatures to a large and gaping ditch. On my right side appeared to be what I now know was an angelic being, and on the left side was a demonic being. In an instant, I was flung over this huge ditch that appeared to have deep water in it; a *very* scary sight for a six year old child.

These beings were at war with each other, both vying to have me on one or the other's side.

Help! Help! I continued to scream, but apparently, not even Main heard me. Surely by now, he'd want me to play with him. Wasn't he at least looking for me? Didn't Jacqueline and some of the others want to play "hide and seek"? And my twin sisters, Barbara and Betty, wouldn't they want to teach me everything that they had learned at school? Where is everybody? My older sister Fannie would be upset because I wasn't present for nap time. Now, I would be in even bigger trouble. And Daddy, he *had* to be looking for his "Gayta." After all, he named me Gaynell and gave me this nickname - Gayta. Somebody please help me!

God was giving me, a little six year old girl, the opportunity to choose. Choose what? A six year old child knows nothing about this kind of thing in a real sense. But even at that young age, He wanted me to know that there are two kingdoms, two sides - good and evil, right and wrong, heaven and hell. What a tremendous realization and responsibility! The reality was that there was a tug of war - pulling and pushing that appeared to last forever and ever. Finally, I was pulled by the angelic figure to the right-hand side of the ditch. I had no idea what had just happened in this spirit realm. Later in life, I came to realize that God had chosen me to live for Him. He wanted me on His side, and there were no ifs, ands, or buts about it.

Finally, my God of the Heavens, allowed me to wake up. "Mama….where's my Mama?" My sisters and brothers were half dressed for church and looking at me as if to question why I wasn't dressed. I felt so strange, so different and just wanted to see my Mama. Finally, I found her in her room….alone. It is unusual for a lady with so many children to have an alone-moment, but there she was in her room getting dressed… tall, beautiful, healthy, and strong. She too looked at me as if to say, "Why aren't you dressed for church?" I didn't care. I was just so glad to see her! I ran and hugged my mother. She was clueless as to what her little girl had just endured. She told me to go get dressed for church. That was alright with me. I didn't tell her about the dream right then and there; my little heart was just so delighted to see her. It made my life, on this side, real again. I ran down the hallway, got dressed, and we all went to church.

What an amazing God that He would teach this important lesson to a young child! Over the years, I have thought about this dream and have wondered why God gave this frightening dilemma to me. I believe God wanted me to know the truth, to know that He is real; that I must choose whom I was going to serve, and live for….my entire life. And you know what, He wants you to KNOW the truth, as well. The truth is what *makes* us *free*! Free to choose and be liberated from death and destruction, hell and the grave.

Have you ever wondered, "Why am I here, and what am I supposed to be doing here on this earth? Do I have a purpose? Where did I come from? What is the *right* choice to make in life's situations? What is the *real* deal? Who really, *is* God? Is it okay to worship Jesus, Mohammed, and Buddha? Aren't they all the same? Help me with these questions because I need truthful answers, you say. I need answers! I need *somebody* to tell me the *truth, NOW!*"

I am so grateful and privileged to be able to share the information in this book with you. This book was birthed one morning while I was in prayer. It was my usual morning prayer before I would go to work, and as I was praying for young people, specifically those in my family, and some others. My heart fell on the fact that they have *so much* to deal with in society these days and have so many forces coming at them with obvious *untruths*. The Lord really showed me the need to be in constant prayer for them, so I wept, and I prayed. During this time, there were some awful, hostile, abominable spirits affecting *my* family and I thought, "Lord, this just can't be.....do something!" And He said, "I have! Now, you do something." My whole-being got quiet before Him, and He showed me this book; not for the young only, but for any and every age, because His Word is from everlasting to everlasting, and from cradle to grave.

His word is for the young, old, black, brown, red, and white. In John 8:32, Jesus said "you shall *know* the truth, and the truth shall *make* you free." For He alone is the way, the truth, and the life. In Him, in His truth, we are *made* free.

Throughout this journey called life, I would be faced with much, and in the back of my mind and the very crevices of my being, I would know right from wrong.

Through the years as I attended or spoke at Sunday school, church, Bible study, conferences, conventions, Christian groups, and organizations, I learned the dire importance of spending time with God. How do you do that, you might ask? Keep reading. I developed a relationship with the Almighty God, the God of my fathers, and the God of the Bible. As you read on, it is my prayer that you will desire and pursue a true *relationship* with God. This is the greatest gift in the entire world.

God Is The Playwright

You are beautiful. You really are. You are somebody special. Don't stop here; read on. No, this is not a "feel good" book, but a message of love from up above....with your name on it.

Do yourself a favor. Take a moment to look up... towards the sky. Whether it is raining or a bright, sunny, true blue kind of day - there is beauty. There's nothing that I love more than to watch the sky after a very fierce thunderstorm. I notice that the sky continues to light up in different sections; the thunder continues to slowly roll and gently moan as the storm moves somewhere else or just dissipates. Ahh, I love it! Psalm 107:28-30 says, "He maketh the storm a calm, so that the waves thereof are still."

And so it is with our lives. Regardless of whether we are sad and misty, or full of joy and happiness, we are all beautiful; each and every one of us, no exceptions.

Your moment of Truth: We ARE because He IS, and if He wasn't, we wouldn't have ever been! He made ALL things good, and that includes you!

I Corinthians 8:6 says, "But to us there is but one God, the Father, of whom are all things, and we in him; and one Lord Jesus Christ, by whom are all things, and we by him."

Let no man......or woman determine who you are, or set your worth or character. For he or she is just a "man" and has not been given that authority by *anyone*. First of all, we all have a divine or God given right to exist, just merely by being born, and to live out all of our days in abundance: abundant health, abundant wealth, and abundant life! No man can take away this divine right, and we are not to give it away either. When almighty God decided that your spirit would be released into this earth, the plan for your life was already set. He downloaded you with His software that contained these powerful words: "Called, Purposed, Fearfully and Wonderfully made....MINE!"

You are called according to His purposes. You are purposed to live, and do the will of God so that you may know and have eternal life. Yes, you are fearfully and wonderfully made. There is no carbon copy of any of us!

I have observed twins now for more than 40 years. I have sisters who are identical twins and they do look alike, are very close, have done many things together, and after all these years, they still like to dress alike, on occasion. But each one is an individual, with her own attributes and her own nature. Each has her own likeness of our natural, earthly father and our heavenly Father.

Yes, you were called to serve God on this earth. Some may say, yes, but I've really blown it; you just don't know. That's why it is important to read God's word. As you read the Bible, you will find story after story where many people had blown it, but God still used them mightily to get His story told and accredited. So, at this point, you haven't blown it too badly with God. Know that unless you have taken your last breath without accepting Jesus as Lord and Savior, you still have time. So now, *get up* and *get in service* for God. Get up! Declare that your builder and maker is God! There's so much grace to run this race, and you will be blessed immeasurably!

Your moment of Truth: You are so fearfully and so wonderfully made. You ARE because He IS. And God alone is the only one that can define you.

When we understand the awesome and ultimate sacrifice that God made for us, then and only then, will we know how precious the gift of Jesus Christ is. His sacrifice was made from total, unselfish, and pure love.

We all need Him. Romans 3:23 says, "All have sinned and fallen short of the glory of God."

Watch for what God will reveal in the days ahead. It will carry real, living excitement!

"In the last days says the Lord, I will pour out of my spirit upon ALL flesh." Not some. ALL – no one will be left out. Not just black or brown flesh. Not just white, red or yellow flesh. ALL flesh! God said in Acts 2:17, "That your sons and your daughters shall prophesy, and your young men shall see visions, and your old men <u>would</u> (not maybe) dream dreams."

Your moment of Truth: God alone is the playwright; He knows your story from beginning to end, and in Him, you win!

This is a promise – a guarantee. Don't give up on your children or even your parents, because God is in all the details for everyone for whom you're praying. God is about to pour out of Himself upon them. If that in itself is not exciting, I don't know what is.

Now, you may get excited when your favorite music artist is releasing a new CD. Well, guess what? He or she and maybe some others will be the only ones truly profiting from it. They get to put the millions in the bank - not you!

Get excited and hear me! At this moment, as God Almighty pours out….pours out of Himself….Ahh…. please *hear* this:

As God pours out Himself, His spirit - nothing in your life will be the same. It will change forever. Light and life will be everywhere reflecting God. Love will reign supreme because He is light, life, and love. That love will cover a multitude of sins – it will overshadow and overtake, and many will be led out of darkness into His marvelous light. God will give out wisdom, witty inventions, money, instruction, provision, and abundance for everything that you need. Godly promises **will** *be fulfilled.*

However, Beloved, you must know and remember that what God gives His own is not for sin. He is to be glorified and His kingdom to be built. The words of the Preacher, our brother and the son of David, king in Jerusalem - Solomon in the Bible, was very candid and transparent when he told us in Ecclesiastes

1:2-4, "Vanity of vanities, saith the Preacher, vanity of vanities; all is vanity. What profit hath a man of all his labour which he taketh under the sun? One generation passeth away, and another generation cometh: but the earth abideth for ever." Yes, it's all vanity (really nothing). Vanity of vanities. And trust me, that brother had it all, nothing lacking. He had wisdom, money, gold, silver, land, cattle of every kind, women of every tribe and nation; yet…he said…it's all vanity…it's really nothing. What a conclusion! What a life!

Yet, there are scores of movie stars, singers, professional athletes, businessmen, politicians, and many others who can identify with a fraction of Solomon's wealth. The Bible says he was the richest man that ever lived and there will never be another like him. And, like Solomon, many trailed off and served other gods. Like some of you, I personally know some who grew up in church, under the teachings of the Holy Bible and the God of Israel. Nevertheless, through the years, the obtaining of wealth and fortune lead them to idol gods through various mediums. Some will admit it and some will not, but the truth of the matter for those who have left the Christian faith, just come back home to the God of the Bible, the God of Abraham, and the God of your fathers.

Never forget that, lest you be deceived by someone working in the enemy's (Satan's) camp, you are being intentionally mislead from the TRUTH of God. That someone could be a person close to you such as your grandmother, mother, father, sibling, teacher, or even a preacher. Know the *truth* of the matter - if *anyone* is trying to rob you of your God given right to be who you were created to be, don't allow it. Don't hear them. Don't listen to them. It's a *lie!*

Instead, choose to live out Psalm 100:1-5 which says, "Make a joyful noise unto the Lord, all ye lands (people). Serve the Lord with gladness: come before his presence with singing. Know ye that the Lord he is God; it is he that hath made us and not we ourselves; we are his people, and the sheep of his pasture. Enter into his gates with thanksgiving, and into his courts with praise; be thankful unto him, and bless his name. For the Lord is good; his mercy is everlasting; and his truth endureth to all generations."

Your moment of Truth: We have not made ourselves. God, the Playwright, the Author and Finisher of our faith, has made us. Our job is to love Him endlessly!

Stop Telling Stories

Jesus says in John 8:44, "Satan is a liar and the father of lies," and this is *truth... Whatever Jesus says is truth!*

Let's talk *truth* about Satan or Lucifer or the Devil. This great deceiver is a created being. See, he likes to get us caught up in a fantasy world; a make believe world, and so often, we fall for it. When I was growing up, my siblings and I were not allowed to say the word "lie" in our household. That's right, that word was too strong. If someone was not telling the truth, we had to say, "Mama, So and So is telling a *"story;"* I did not do what she claimed that I did." When in reality, So and So was telling a *lie*.

Except, that's exactly what Satan does all the time - tells us a seemingly believable *story (lie)*, and once we believe it, we act on it and are sadly deceived. He has told many of us that, "O*h for* **sure** *the grass is greener on the other side," (he hasn't even been to the other side)!* How many times have we thought - how in the world did I get *here?* He knows that many of us have problems differentiating between truths and lies. Why? Simply because we don't take the time to read the truth – the Word of God - for ourselves. If you don't know the truth, yes, you will believe and act on a lie. It is the truth that *makes* us free!

On the Mt. of Olives, Jesus declared as is written in John 8:36, "If the Son therefore shall make you free, ye shall be free indeed."

Your moment of Truth: We're not just free in our words, but in our deeds as well.

Then there's the *little white lie*. Wait a minute....hold up! Does the fact that the *story* you are telling is *little* or *white* make it alright to do? God forbid. When we allow this kind of thinking and action, we simply are being deceived.

I can remember when I graduated from a historically black college, after which I went to work for a major insurance company in a predominantly white community in the hills of Western Maryland. Many of my female co-workers used the expression, "Oh, it was just a little white lie; he didn't mean any harm". A lie always means harm, whether it is to a person or to God. In Genesis 20:2-18, when Abraham was allowed to say that Sarah was his sister, it caused great problems. Another man almost took his wife, not sister, to be *his* wife. Let us take a look at the *"scriptures:"*

2. And Abraham said of Sarah his wife, She is my sister: and Abimelech king of Gerar sent, and took Sarah.

3. But God came to Abimelech in a dream by night, and said to him, Behold, thou art but a dead man, for the woman which thou hast taken; for she is a man's wife.

4. But Abimelech had not come near her: and he said, Lord, wilt thou slay also a righteous nation?

5. Said he not unto me, She is my sister? and she, even

she herself said, He is my brother: in the integrity of my heart and innocency of my hands have I done this.

6. And God said unto him in a dream, Yea, I know that thou didst this in the integrity of thy heart; for I also withheld thee from sinning against me: therefore suffered I thee not to touch her.

7. Now therefore restore the man his wife; for he is a prophet, and he shall pray for thee, and thou shalt live: and if thou restore her not, know thou that thou shalt surely die, thou, and all that are thine.

8. Therefore Abimelech rose early in the morning, and called all his servants, and told all these things in their ears: and the men were sore afraid.

9. Then Abimelech called Abraham, and said unto him, What hast thou done unto us? and what have I offended thee, that thou hast brought on me and on my kingdom a great sin? thou hast done deeds unto me that ought not to be done.

10. And Abimelech said unto Abraham, What sawest thou, that thou hast done this thing?

11. And Abraham said, Because I thought, Surely the fear of God is not in this place; and they will slay me for my wife's sake.

12. And yet indeed she is my sister; she is the daughter

of my father, but not the daughter of my mother; and she became my wife.

13. And it came to pass, when God caused me to wander from my father's house, that I said unto her, This is thy kindness which thou shalt shew unto me; at every place whither we shall come, say of me, He is my brother.

14. And Abimelech took sheep, and oxen, and menservants, and womenservants, and gave them unto Abraham, and restored him Sarah his wife.

15. And Abimelech said, Behold, my land is before thee: dwell where it pleaseth thee.

16. And unto Sarah he said, Behold, I have given thy brother a thousand pieces of silver: behold, he is to thee a covering of the eyes, unto all that are with thee, and with all other: thus she was reproved.

17. So Abraham prayed unto God: and God healed Abimelech, and his wife, and his maidservants; and they bare children.

18. For the LORD had fast closed up all the wombs of the house of Abimelech, because of Sarah Abraham's wife.

I am sure that Abraham did not want to lie, but because of fear of what might have happened to him and his wife, he chose to lie.

It is true in life that we may tell lies, whether we think

they are little or white lies, they are still lies. *Always* quickly repent and don't make it a way of life. Most lies are told out of fear; fear of rejection or the response of others. Remember that in Luke 12:5, the Bible tells us to fear God more than man, and to fear him who is able to place you in heaven or hell more than flesh and blood.

The Bible says that Jesus is the way, the truth and the life. So, that makes Satan, the deceiver, the liar, and the death angel. What an opportunity we have in Christ Jesus; we can live an abundant life here on earth, enjoying the sweet peace of God when we allow truth to prevail. Lies can bring drama, confusion, and sometimes unwanted and everlasting pain. Let us live this life in truth and victory that has already been provided by Jesus at the cross. He did **not** die in vain, but instead for you and for me so that we might do as the Bible says in Galatians 1:4, "Escape from this present evil world, according to the will of God and our Father."

Your moment of Truth: We ought to fear God much more than man in our daily lives. Be very quick to repent of lies or any type of sin.

Knowing Who You Are

You see, the *truth* of the matter is that you are special, beautifully, fearfully and wonderfully made. You are made in God's image - not just anybody's image - not Hollywood's image; but in the image of the Almighty God.

Who could be more beautiful than he who is made in the image of God? Have you ever observed the freshly fallen snow or the picturesque blue sky as a backdrop for huge, fluffy clouds? Have you ever taken the time to look at the trees in the fall of the year, whose leaves turn into beautiful, brilliant colors? Have you felt the peace and calm when it's raining outside watering God's earth.

My favorite gift from God is the beautiful, deep blue sea. Who can know its depth, but God? Who can count its inhabitants, creatures large and small, but God? Who can know all the awesome shades of blue and seafoam green, but God? Awesome - isn't it?

As a family, we have often gone on Caribbean cruises, and I can recall having a great time with my nieces and nephews while riding wave runners in the open ocean. On one occasion, we went out as far as the lifeguards would allow. We noticed that the colors of the water changed so many times from blue to deep blue, turquoise to green, and back to blue. Just magnificent! We could see straight down into the sea, as far as the naked eye could see.

Furthermore, have you looked in the mirror lately? That's right, you look just like he wanted you too. He wants to use that man, that woman, that you see in the mirror! Ahh, the beauty and the majesty of our Creator!

You see, *Genesis 1:1 says, "In the beginning God created the heaven and the earth".* That same God, creator of heaven and earth said in *Genesis 1:26-27, "…let us make man (you) in our own image, After our likeness; and let them have dominion over the fish of the sea, and over the fowl of the air, and over the cattle, and over all the earth, and every creeping thing that creepeth upon the earth. So God* **created** *man in his own image, in the image of God created he him;* **male** *and* **female created** *He them".*

Your moment of Truth: Let no man define you; God already has.

Do you hear what He's saying? *You* were created in His image. You didn't just happen, and you're not a mistake. And you're not made in the likeness of an ape! No! You have been given *dominion, rule*, and *ownership* over animals, birds, fish, etc, and that includes apes! How can you be an ape when God has given you dominion over all apes!!

If you believe the Word of God, you'll know that you are not and did not descend from an ape. Instead, you were created in the likeness of Almighty God creator of heaven and earth! Whether Jew or Gentile, Black, White, Asian, Latino, Christian, Muslim, Hindu, etc. - you were **created** in His image and none other.

Satan would have us believing lies instead of God's truth. First, he wants us not to believe where God said we came from nor how God said we got here. Secondly, he lies when he says that one ethnic group is better or superior to another. Now, on ethnicity or race, the Bible is **very** clear. Either the Bible is true (and it is) or it's not. In Genesis 6:5-7, we read that due to men's evil hearts...God destroyed the earth (which is where we still live today), by a great flood (water), except Noah, his family, and the specified animals that God asked him to keep in the ark. Genesis 6:10 states that Noah begat or caused to have birthed three sons, Shem, Ham and Japheth, brothers, not lords and masters - one over the other. Next, when the flood was over, Noah, his wife, the animals and the *same* three sons, Shem, Ham, and Japheth, brothers (along with their wives), emerged from the ark and inhabited the earth. **All** other men had been destroyed off of the earth.

Once the Great Flood was over and the earth was dry again, Gen. 9:18, 19 states, "And the sons of Noah, that went forth off the ark, were Shem, and Ham, and Japheth: and Ham is the father of Canaan. These are the three sons of Noah: and of *them* was the whole earth overspread." Noah's family were the only people on the earth since the earth and all of its human inhabitants had been destroyed by water from the Great Flood. Therefore, now we all know where we came from: one of these three brothers.

When I lived in Detroit, Michigan, I had a wonderful Jewish business associate and friend (cousin really, based on Gen 9:18,19) named David. On one occasion my friend had just returned from Israel and wanted to share his photos with me during a business luncheon. As we viewed his vacation pictures, he explained where he had visited in Israel, the various temples and mountains, and all the beautiful Bible stuff over there. I stopped him and said, "You know it isn't fair - with slavery and the evils that were committed against Black families, we don't know who we are or from whom we descended. You, on the other hand, know what tribe of Israel you're from and of whom you descended" With really stern, but loving brown eyes, he looked at me and asked, "Didn't you go to Sunday school and read the Bible when you were young?" I said, "Yes, of course, my mother made us go every Sunday." With the same caring look, he said, "Then you *know* who you are". So, we left it at that.

I never, ever forgot our conversation and through the years would often ponder it. God, through the truth of his awesome Word, has made it so clear and plain…. that now…..I *know* who I am! It is ONLY in God and His awesome Word that we can know who we are and live out the purpose for which we were created.

What an awesome *truth* that *no one* can change or take away from you. Please do not allow politicians, school teachers, scientists, deceptive ministries, or anyone else to turn you away from God's Truth – His Word. They have their thoughts and philosophies and you have Truth! Choose to believe man minimally, but *always* believe God fully. You can trust Him!

Your moment of Truth: Many times in this life, what we become is not a result of what we were created to be, but of our own choosing.

God's Created Woman
Of Virtue

Hear ye, hear ye! Girls, women, young ladies! May I *please* have your undivided attention for a few minutes? I must warn you of an attack. To some, it has already occurred and to others, this is your opportunity to be on the lookout. Are you listening? Please, please do!

There is a thief and liar among us. He's not just stealing, but assaulting, robbing, even murdering to literally TAKE what God gave to *you* only. Your very *womanhood* is under attack! You're one of God's most beautiful creations on this earth and my, are you purposed. Do you remember Genesis 1:27, "…..male and *female* created he them." God created a girl or a woman….. female. Not half and half and not to be or act like a man or a male, but female.

You see, if you're a girl or a woman, God *decided* that you would be female, and the decision stands. I know, I know, our world says otherwise, and so we think that it's okay. Television says it's okay. Some musical renderings say it's okay. Hollywood says it's okay, but what does God say on this matter?

We don't have the right to change it, but just as Satan came to Adam and Eve with a lie, he has come to many precious females with the same lie. Listen, "You don't have to accept it." Choose to be the woman that God needs you to be in this hour in which we live. You will be so much happier and fulfilled that you uniquely walk in His peace, and your need to follow the crowd will diminish. You are an extraordinary woman because God made you that way!

Your moment of Truth: God's decisions are sovereign, and we don't have the right to change them. Live free in your created purpose!

Being a woman is your created nature. God, the awesome Creator, made a decision to create Adam or **man**. Then, He decided that it was not good for man to be alone. He then decided that He would make a help meet for the **man.** So, what did He do next? The Bible says in Genesis 2:21-23, "And God caused a deep sleep to fall upon Adam, and he slept; and He took one of his ribs, and closed up the flesh instead thereof; and the rib, which the Lord God had taken from man, made He a **woman,** and brought her unto the man."

Wow! Did you see that? What an awesome Creator! And Adam said, "This is now bone of my bones, and flesh of my flesh: *she* shall be called Woman, because she was taken out of Man." Adam knew that the **woman** had been taken out of the man…Eve had been taken out of him! God could have made Eve just like Adam, but he didn't. He made her a **female**, having taken her *out* of Adam. Whew!

Sometimes you may not feel as pretty as another girl or woman. Someone may have even called you ugly. When I look in the mirror, I proclaim: "I am God's beauty queen." I share this with many young ladies and girls. I tell them to say it aloud, and make sure the devil hears it. Then it doesn't matter what others think of your looks. You will be confident that you are beautifully, fearfully, and wonderfully made! You will say it, and believe it!

You know why? God's standards of beauty are much higher than that of Hollywood or society's. He made you with splendor, wonder, excellence, and majesty. He kissed you with wisdom and bathed you in love. He created you with curly or straight hair, light or dark skin, big or small hips, short or tall stature - to represent the kingdom of God and not that of darkness. Get in that mirror daily and declare who you are, and go out and have a victorious day every day! I don't worry about my looks. I *know* that I am beautiful...... I am God's beauty queen. I have a niece that I call my Pretty Baby. I always tell her that she's pretty inside and out. I didn't know that a few years later, she, like so many others, would need these very words to know that she was special, and, to overcome some of life's obstacles. I pray that in some way, I have made all of my nieces and nephews feel special, because they are. Encourage others in love that they too may love God, themselves, and others just the way He made them.

Satan has tricked so many into thinking that we are our own and we can do whatever we want to do because it's our thing. Wrong!

We were created for God's use and purpose. Genesis 2:7 says, "And the Lord *formed* man of the dust of the ground, and *breathed* into his nostrils the breath of life; and man *became* a living soul." **God breathed His breath into each and every one of us!** Without God's breath, we cease to exist.

Even though we have God's breath, Satan tries to mislead us through our eyes, ears, and even tries to breathe down our throats! Ladies, we have to *decide* that he's a liar and that we want to live for God, the one whose very breath dwells within us.

Your moment of Truth: No matter what the world tells us, God made a woman for man and man for a woman.

The enemy, Satan, would like to blind, lie to, and deceive every one of us. God gave us His Word (the Holy Bible), gave us Jesus (who died for our sins), and Jesus sent His Holy Spirit to comfort us. With all of these precious gifts and weaponry, we are armed to *choose* life and not be deceived. That very breath that God breathed into us becomes alive, and we are not deceived. Jesus has overcome death, hell, and the grave for us! He is our redeemer, and therefore we can have eternal life with Him.

Life on earth is so temporal, so short, just a vapor. I remember when my daddy went to be with the Lord. Oh, my whole world was changed in an instant. You see, regardless of his shortcomings, I loved my daddy with all of my heart, and he meant so much to the whole family. He had always been the provider, along with my mother, and the leader of our family. On Christmas morning at the Jones' house, you did not jump out of bed and open presents, but instead, you went to church. Daddy, Mother, and all of us first went to bless the Lord at church. After that, we could have our fun-time and toy-time by opening our Christmas presents! We all still love Christmas and are so thankful for its true meaning: A savior, our Savior was born and lives forevermore. He is alive!

Losing Daddy was like losing a part of my heart and soul. There were days that I really didn't feel like continuing this journey called life. In my heart, I knew that I had to let him go, but I didn't want to do that. I wanted him back on this earth with me; with the family where I thought he belonged. God began to show me that Daddy had fulfilled his time and purpose on earth and that it was time for him to be with his heavenly Father. I was weeping for him one day in my dining room and all of a sudden, I felt a strong angelic presence. The voice simply said, "*Just let him go, it is well.*" That day, God got my attention and although I still long for him sometimes, *I've let him go* from this earth. It's okay to miss somebody or a thing, but let's not *hold* them. Some of us do this with our former spouses resulting in the inability to move on with our lives. God needs us to move on if we are going to be of good service to His kingdom and purpose in this hour.

You see, we have a purpose to be fulfilled in *this* time. We can't stop or die in our wilderness experiences which can include the death of a loved one, divorce, depression, or disappointment. We have to seek the Father to know and walk in our purpose. I would not be writing this book if God did not purpose it for my life in this time. Quite frankly, I've wasted enough time. No more wasted time for me. You see, I don't know exactly when *my* appointment is going to be!

Your moment of Truth: We are in *this* time to fulfill God's purposes for our lives. The Lord has need of you!

Inside of every girl is a woman, created by God in His image with a purpose to fulfill. And inside of every woman is a girl that longs to have a relationship with her Heavenly Father, her "Daddy", her Creator.

I know that sometimes life brings heartache and pain and we feel that others just don't understand us or our choices. I know that love doesn't always come easily. It can be lacking from parents, siblings, the opposite sex, and in many other areas. Many of us know people who've never met their mother or their father. This is very painful and sometimes they blame themselves. Don't blame yourself! Your heavenly father is always there for you no matter what, but you have to allow Him to be your "Daddy" because Psalm 68:5 says that, "A father of the fatherless, and a judge of the widows, is God in his holy habitation. Don't resist His love and he will heal your hurts and make you whole. He is the Lover of your soul!

Sometimes we have parents who are unloving in their acts towards us. This is when we pray, "Lord, I need your grace to love my mother or my father, or even a sibling." A relationship with God and a prayer life is so important right now and in these last days in which we are living. God is so easy to talk to, and He doesn't care if you cry, stutter, scream, yell, sing, pout, etc., - just let Him hear from you on a regular basis. The more we talk to and listen to God, the more we will know His voice and will ignore the voice of the stranger, Satan.

Although I experienced love from my parents and siblings while growing up, I also *knew* that attacks could come from anyone at any time. Understand something: Satan doesn't care who he uses to get you out of the will and purpose that God has for your life. He just wants to make sure that you are distracted and miss the mark. However, remember your relationship with God. You can talk to Him whenever the need arises and you can ask for the wisdom and the grace to deal with your troubles.

Don't, *do unto them as they do unto you.* The Word is right when it instructs us to keep the wise sayings of the Golden Rule in Matthew 7:12, " Therefore all things whatsoever ye would that men should do to you, do ye even so to them: for this is the law and the prophets."

Your moment of Truth: A relationship with God and a prayer life are vital for mere survival in these last days in which we are living. Form yours today!

God's Created Man Of Valor

Can you imagine my two (2) brothers growing up with thirteen (13) sisters? I have often been asked, "How in the world did those two boys survive with all of those girls?" My answer has been consistent through the years, as I would answer with "Very well because they were spoiled. The girls had their chores and the boys had theirs." Elbert, Jr. and Jimmy would wrestle and fight with each other, but never really with the girls. They were good boys, never giving my parents too much trouble. They were allowed some different freedoms than the girls such as staying out later at the ballpark or a party. The girls on the other hand, had a curfew that had to be kept or we would be in lots of trouble. All my brothers had to do was explain where they were and why they were late.

One thing my parents realized was that the boys would grow up to be men, and they didn't plan to raise any wimps. They knew that God had given them boys *and* girls, not all the same. My brothers played sports which helped to make them tough. They also learned mechanics and carpentry which would lend to them becoming family leaders and providers. The girls were raised mostly with domestic skills. Working at the family businesses taught us good work ethics and responsibilities. Also, it taught us a sense of community and helping those less fortunate, especially working at our family store - Jones Supermarket. Afterall, God's Word does say that if a man doesn't work, he should not eat. I did not say it, God did!

We know from Genesis that God created Adam and placed him in the Garden of Eden, and later gave him a beautiful woman named Eve. Before Eve came on the scene, it was made known to Adam that he was head of household. Eve was to be his helper. Each person had a purpose.

I believe it is so vital for children to be raised in the fear and admonition of the Lord. And since we are talking about boys who will one day become men, we are going to focus on them and the valor in which God intends for them to walk. Without God, it is impossible to walk in their intended valor and strength, making them more vulnerable to the enemy's tricks and robbery. I often look at young boys and pray for them on the spot, asking God to make them the men that He intends for them to become, to let every purpose in their lives be fulfilled for God's kingdom.

We need the men to lead as God intended. I know that there are some strong sisters out there be they politicians, attorneys, doctors, or other, but God's intent has always been for men to lead. Satan knows this and does everything that he can to try to stop the plan of God. He never will, but that doesn't stop him from trying and placing stumbling blocks in the lives of our precious boys and men. Satan knows that if men get out of position and God's purpose that oftentimes women will do similarly, and children will follow. He hates the family and God's plan for strength, commitment, success, love and respect, and does everything that he can to cause derailment.

Some men carry the pain of an abused boy within them, and this causes a lot of pain that they live with daily. I have good news for you precious boy and man, there is healing in the blood of Jesus! You don't have to live in shame, hurt, defeat, and with a plan to hurt others. You can be healed and set free from your hurts and pains. You are so loved by the Father, and He is the one who makes you clean and whole again. He desperately wants us to keep our minds stayed on Him and He *will* keep us in perfect peace: *Peace* to pursue God and His plan for your life, not the enemy's plan. You would be amazed at the restoration that only God can bestow upon your life and cause you to smile again, to laugh again, and to feel completely whole again! Though you may have received a severe punch, God wants you to *get up* and go on with the journey that He has laid out for your life. Don't become full of bitterness, rage, and revenge. The person or persons who hurt you have not gotten off God's radar, and

He says in Romans 12:19, "Dearly beloved, avenge not yourselves, but rather give place unto wrath: for it is written, Vengeance is mine; I will repay, saith the Lord." He allows rain to fall and the sun to shine on both the just and the unjust, but His excellency is not to be mistaken for seeing Him as not paying attention. He knows and sees everything and has not forgotten your case.

One of the most powerful things that you can do is work to build a relationship with Almighty God. Next, reach out and help others who have been abused, misused, or perhaps they just had it rough in life. I am a woman who desperately wanted a child and a boy in particular. I had envisioned raising my children very similarly, to how I had been raised. I had looked forward to teaching them God's word and His plan for their lives according to the Bible. Although I didn't get that opportunity naturally so, I have done many things to enhance the spiritual lives of my nephews. I tell them who they are and that God has a plan for their lives as men. I have reminded them that their great grandfather was a Baptist preacher and loved the God of the Bible.

Boys and men, as long as you have breath in your body, you can call upon the name of the Lord and He will save you and heal you. God is madly in love with you and wants to teach and train you just as a loving earthly father would. Don't dismiss Him just because someone else was unlovely. Even if you grew up without an earthly father either inside or outside the home, or perhaps you have never even been told who your father is, you have a heavenly Father who loves you unconditionally. He's waiting to teach and train you as His own – a man of valor. God does not want you to join gangs who are empty inside and hurt others. He wants to show you a better way for your life. He just needs you to show up for class, so get going!

In II Chronicles 7:14, God says "If my people, which are called by my name, shall humble themselves, and pray, and seek my face, and turn from their wicked ways; then will I hear from heaven, and will forgive their sin, and will heal their land." God is gracious my brother. Whether you are white, black, yellow, red, or brown, God will heal your land. He will open doors that you never thought could be open unto you. Every board room in America and around the world can be changed at the hand of God. That business that you desire to start, He wants you to start it too. That woman of virtue that you desire for a wife. He is just waiting on you to "get in His face", to seek Him with all of your heart. If you will take the time to pray and develop a relationship with Almighty God, read and study His Word, wait on Him and trust Him, I know you will *suddenly* experience awesome and amazing changes in your life.

Your moment of Truth: God had many men of valor throughout the Bible. Moses, Joshua, David, Daniel, and He wants to add your name to the roll.

Whose Helpmeet, Lord?

Have you ever said "Lord, am I *ever* going to be someone's help meet? Am I ever going to get married?" I have heard many women declare that they have boycotted weddings until they become the bride. If you have felt this way, you are not alone. Loneliness and feeling alone are no fun and can surely wear on your measure of patience. Notice, I said **patience** or the ability to wait with endurance and not complain. It is perseverance of suffering with calmness and self-control.

Many will say, "You just don't know, I don't have any patience." Yes, you do! You have to exercise it, and it will grow. I am a living witness. There are many things in life, such as designer purses, expensive cars and homes, that we feel we must have right now. Not! This mindset has gotten us into so much trouble, and guess what? It takes *patience* to get us out of it. For instance, if you make too many purchases on your credit cards, it will take a while (patience) to pay them off. If you get involved with the wrong person (somebody who is not intended to be your helpmeet), it will take patience to get away from them and eventually forget about them.

Subsequently, the lesson here is to exercise patience on the front end to avoid the *mandatory* patience on the latter end.

I can remember years ago when I really, really wanted a child but had problems conceiving. A dear and wonderful friend named Almeda Monroe-Turner was visiting me during that time and said something so profound: "Don't be discouraged…, you know, we all want something from the Lord." Just hearing her say that helped me to take my eyes off my need and to see the needs of others.

Almeda loved the Lord, was single at the time, and desired to be married. Unlike me, she grew up expressing herself very vocally, many times with no holds barred. Oftentimes, we would agree in prayer over various world events, pray for the peace of Jerusalem, pray for all seven continents, pray for our pastors, their families and our churches, our cities and for one another. I prayed that the Lord would cause her intended husband to "find" her – Proverbs 18:22, "Whoso findeth a wife findeth a good thing, and obtaineth favour of the Lord." She would pray for me. "Lord, children are a heritage unto you; give her a child to be brought up in the fear and admonition of the Lord." Psalm 127:3 says, "Lo, children are an heritage of the Lord: and the fruit of the womb is his reward." Oh, we'd pray and pray and pray. And we believed God, too. However, sometimes I would become discouraged when month after month, nothing happened; no "bun was in the oven." I must share that God was certainly faithful, and I did become pregnant. That pregnancy ended in miscarriage, but after all the sadness that I experienced, God stamped in my heart that He was indeed able. I cannot explain why I do not have natural children, but I do know that my God continues to keep me in reverent amazement, and I totally trust Him. I had some dark days which we will talk about in another book, but life is too precious to waste time questioning God. The fact that He knows *far* more than we do, and so much more, is just one of the things that makes Him God!

I firmly believe that God has someone for everyone, and He has made no mistake in doing so. There certainly may be present day eunuchs and those who do not desire to ever be married. For those who do desire a husband or a wife, God has one for them. You only need *one* person of God's choosing. "How can I know when it's God's choosing," you might ask? Once again, having that relationship with God, praying – talking to Him on a consistent basis will keep you in communion with Him as He orders your steps, leads, and guides you. Usually, we are the ones who get out of step with God's plan and decide to do our own thing. Oh boy, here comes that mandatory patience!

One thing that I have prayed about and always wished, is that older people would be more candid about relationships; good ones and bad ones. Everyone is often so tight-lipped, when many times, if you share; someone might possibly avoid pitfalls and unnecessary blunders and heartache.

Your moment of Truth: James 1:4, "But let patience have her perfect work, that you may be perfect and entire, wanting nothing."

A life lesson that I have learned is that I could have chosen ten men and lined them up. One of them may have been *good* for me and another one *better*, but my Father would always know which one is the absolute best for me. I didn't say perfect because that doesn't exist, but I said the *best* one for me. How does He know? Because He created the man and me, He knows exactly what each of our needs are and how we can live for Him and complement one another once we are together.

The world currently fosters a philosophy that God is not needed in human affairs. What a lie, and what a mistake! We cannot even breathe without God. What ignorance to think that if you need God to even breathe, wouldn't you need Him to make major decisions in your life? Think about this, if we just want to be downright "religious," don't we at least need Him to make *big* decisions in our lives?

The truth to be told is that in Him, we live and move and have our very being. Personally, I must have him in all of my affairs, every one of them. I have made enough mistakes by choosing on my own and sometimes listening to other people. When you take the time to spend time with God, you'll *know* Him; *know* His voice and hear Him so clearly. John 10:27-28 says, "My sheep hear my voice, and I know them, and they follow me: And I give unto them eternal life; and they shall never perish, neither shall any man pluck them out of my hand."

It is amazing how we are transformed into people who listen and follow Him as opposed to those who blindly blunder through this life saying, "Lord, please let us make the right decisions." He wants you to make the right decisions, and trust me, He's a gentleman and will not overstep your will.

Beloved, just make up your mind that you want Him to lead and guide you into *all* truths, and that you want His Word to be a lamp unto your feet and a light unto your path. One thing I *know* for sure is that He'll *never* lead you in the wrong path. If you should take yourself off the path, repent and hurry up and get back on the right one.

What I love so much about God is His simplicity. Because He loves us and knows that some of us may get off the path at times, He simply says in His Word to "call upon me and I will answer." Isn't that sweet? *"Call…..upon Me…..and I WILL answer."*

Beloved, we don't ever have to give up or throw in the towel. Know that when we are at our lowest moment or weakest point, find the strength to "call" upon the Lord with assurance that He WILL answer. Satan tries to make us think, "Whew, we've really blown it this time, and there's no turning back to God". *Liar, liar, liar.* God can't wait to hear from *you.* The Word says that if "God saves us, then we shall be saved; if God heals us, then we shall be healed." I believe that if he delivers us, then we shall be delivered; and if he hears us, then we shall be heard.

Your moment of Truth: God is truly the Father who never fails. He has healed all of our diseases and forgiven all of our sins. Satan is a liar and totally unreliable.

Having gone through a divorce during the "second phase" of my life was difficult and most interesting. I am talking about having to face difficult situations that I never, ever had planned! Sometimes, in areas that you think you are strong, you find out that you are weak. Conversely, in areas where you think you may be weak, you will find that He has made you much stronger than you thought. In our weakness, He is strong! I am convinced that it takes loving and seeking God everyday to live the victorious life, whether you are married or single.

Always know that God really does care about you and every issue that you have to deal with daily. Our brother Solomon told us in Ecclesiastes 1:9, that there is *nothing* new under the sun. Nothing! Sometimes you may feel so alone, and may think that you are the only person going through particular challenges; but there is absolutely nothing new under the sun! Solomon was deemed the wisest man that ever lived, certainly he knew a lot.

We must always remember that we are not our own and that our bodies are the temple of the Holy Spirit. The world has had an all too famous slang expression, "It's Your *Thang,* Do What You Want To Do." You know what I've learned in this life…..it's really not "*My Thang."* I can be silenced by death or rendered dysfunctional by disease, but I would still call upon the Lord.

Thank God that He hears me when I call upon Him, lifts me up when I've fallen, and leads and guides me by His Holy Spirit. He loves me so much. I thank God that it's a "*Love Thang*" between Him and me; between Him and you. Satan cannot take that away unless you just hand it over to him allowing robbery.

Again, if we allow Him, God, by His precious Holy Spirit will always lead and guide us into all truths. It is not His will for us to stumble and fall, and keep on stumbling and falling-over and over, and over. Instead, He has need of us. We are to be empowered in prayer and relationship with Him so that we can help others. Woman, you are to be strengthened to help another sister. Man, you are to be strengthened to help pull up another brother. Now is the time to take our positions in the kingdom to please God. It is crucial in this hour. We cannot depend or wait on the government to "bail us out". We are already FREE!! The work that Jesus did on the cross is finished. What are we waiting for? Let's get moving! Let's not let another sister or brother live without the good news of the Gospel of Jesus Christ, suffer in sin, go hungry, or suffer in poverty.

My prayer is that we boldly, on a daily basis, tell someone the truth of the glorious Gospel of Jesus Christ, that he or she may be free. Regardless of skin color, every man, woman, boy and girl, was created by the Almighty God and has a soul. He or she is in need of the Savior.

As we witness and share the good news of the Gospel with others, let us be fully persuaded and confident of the assurance of salvation that we have in Christ Jesus. What an awesome thing!

What's So Good About Grace?

In my life, I have learned so much about grace. I've often told many of my friends and relatives that my name or at least my middle name should have been Grace. That's just how good God has been to me, and how great a love He's shown me all of my life. Grace is one of those attributes that's almost too good to be true!

Has anyone ever given money to you or done a favor for no reason without your asking? Now, that's grace! It is unmerited favor and the love of God toward mankind. I like to sum it up as God just loves me and loves making me smile! So many times He could have ended my life "just like that." He could have allowed me to be in many accidents or have illnesses, and the list goes on. Instead, He has just shown so much love toward me!

I believe that many of you have similar stories and have been so very blessed beyond measure. And even if you have different stories, you are still here for a reason… to start living new and victorious lives today! It is time to live the story and tell others of God's grace and mercy! Salvation is not selfish, but we are to plant and water, and plant and water, and God *will* give the increase! It is not about us; not about the preacher; not about your favorite seat at church (the one that you don't want anyone else to sit in). Remember, it is all for the kingdom! Only what we do for Christ will last. Everything else is very temporary.

One of the saddest realities to me is sometimes seeing the Church of the Lord Jesus Christ looking just like Corporate America. Having spent twenty plus years in Corporate America, there are so many things that don't look anything like God. And many times, so it is with the church. Who told us that it's okay to not love because of skin color? Corporate America, many times, will not promote because of skin color. Can I get real? Folks, it's time for truth, and there isn't much time left to tell it. I've gone to many church conferences across America, and there were absolutely no minority speakers, but half the audience may have been minorities. Why is this happening? Today, there are still many churches that you may decide to visit where you may get stared at for just about the entire service. I know that I'm fearfully and wonderfully made, but really, the entire service? For those of you that may stare at worshippers in your church simply because they don't look like you, please stop it! Some of you are much more receptive to a fellow parishioner bringing a dog to church and cooing over how cute he is, than another soul who may not know Jesus, but whose soul may need saving at that time. Is it about the kingdom or us? We need to choose to live by Godly principles because the Lord is certainly coming soon.

Each of us needs to go out of our way to embrace others with the love of Christ. We are commanded to "love our neighbors as ourselves." Somehow, we have been bewitched into thinking that it's okay not to love our neighbor if they don't look like us. This has to stop! We need to become "God pleasers" rather than "man pleasers". When we do that, we will be much more fulfilled, happy, and we will please God. His kingdom enlarges as the Sons of God are made manifest in the earth. We are to live, whether in church or out of church, to the glory of God.

Be a true worshipper of the one true God. John 4:24 says that, "God is a Spirit: and they that worship him must worship him in spirit and in truth." God is not playing, and we shouldn't be either.

Two very simple keys which I've learned in this life that will truly bless your lives are:

> **Worshipping God** – this is a daily delight that each of us should take time to do. Make sure to spend some quality time with the Lord - just you and Him. If you're married, you and your spouse certainly can do this together. Never get angry or upset with anyone because they are not willing to worship. YOU do it no matter what!

God knows the voice of each person which He created, and He wants to hear your voice. Not the choir, praise team, or usher board, but your voice. Talk to Him; HOLLA! Call on His name, sing him a song, praise His Holy Name, let Him know that you're so glad that He saved you and loves you. Let Him know that you love Him back. Show gratitude and thank Him for all things, great and small. The more gratitude you show, the more reasons you'll have to show gratitude. You will be so glad that you did, and you will find that your problems or cares will leave your mind. Then your mind will begin to stay on the Lord. He will keep you in perfect peace. He will deal with each of your problems, no matter what! God said that if we keep our minds stayed on Him, He will keep us in perfect peace. Isaiah 26:3 tells us, "Thou wilt keep him in perfect peace, whose mind is stayed on thee: because he trusteth in thee." Peace is priceless! God's peace is perfect peace! This is true! This is real! Beloved, if only we would just trust Him, and take Him at His word!

1 Peter 5:7 says, "Casting all your care upon him; for he careth for you." We're commanded to cast our cares on the Lord, for He truly careth for us.

Sometimes, just lie quietly before Him, and allow Him to speak to your very being. It is so wonderful, so powerful. We often think that this is what the preacher is supposed to be doing. No, those that name the name of Christ should be doing this daily, or as often as possible. Can you imagine how much power each of us would have, and the power that the church collectively would have if we spent more personal time with God? We would be unstoppable and provoke the world to jealousy. People who may not know the Lord or have a relationship with Him would start to hunger and thirst to know Him. I know that we would see far more salvations, deliverances, and miracles.

- **Become a Giver** – Luke 6:38 shares the good news for you to give, and it shall be given unto you; good measure, pressed down, and shaken together, and running over, shall men give into your bosom. For with the same measure that ye mete withal it shall be measured to you again. Wow! God could simply say, give, because I said so, or give, because I've given to you. No, once again, an extension of His awesome GRACE is available to you! I know what's so good about grace!

As a cheerful giver, I could tell you countless stories about how God has blessed me over the years. It would take the rest of this book and twenty more to tell it all. As a young girl, I would sometimes attend church with my grandmother. I'd often hear the older people singing, "You can't beat God's giving, no matter how you try,..." I'm a living witness that song and its lyrics are so very true.

One such story that I will share with you is my life's journey as an employee at different places with different companies. God has always promoted me and given me a higher income than the prior job. I worked in Corporate America for twenty years for a certain company, and my income was great. I had no real complaints. My salary was quite sufficient as I was paid according to my knowledge and skills. After resigning and working several years in a different industry, I found myself going back to my original industry. God provided nearly three times the income that I had made prior to leaving the industry the first time. Amazing!

He is so true to His word.

Some in the church find themselves questioning: should we tithe or should we not? Is tithing for today? Is tithing just for the Jews? How can I give when I only have just a little myself? Folks, as we have already discussed, **when you worship God, you don't have to care about money.** You will begin to find it easy to give. You will want to give. Not just at church, but anywhere: at the supermarket, on the street, at restaurants, and wherever God leads you. I am a living witness that your cup will stay in the overflow. We serve a gracious God. Oh, if we would just love, and trust Him!

Remember that Stuff - all of it - belongs to Him. He says in Psalm 24:1, "The earth is the LORD'S, and the fulness thereof; the world, and they that dwell therein." It all belongs to Him. When you (in obedience to His word) give, your blessings from your Father just continue to be released to you in abundance. There is no lack in the Lord.

One final note, when you give, remember to do so as unto the Lord. If you don't feel comfortable with the people in charge or what the ministry or whomever does with the money, ask God to lead you. He will give you wisdom in this matter, even if it means that you have to attend another place of worship. It is all about the kingdom. However, if you give, but you just don't trust because giving is new for you, know that you are in obedience to God's word, and He will honor that. Corinthians 9:7 says, "Every man according as he purposeth in his heart, so let him give; not grudgingly, or of necessity: for God loveth a cheerful giver." Don't allow others to cause you to miss out on your blessings.

Say Goodbye, Let Yesterday Die

Do you know that God lives in the now? He is an ever *present* God and lives in the *today*. Yesterday is gone…...FOREVER. Only He knows if tomorrow is coming, and even if tomorrow comes, who says that you, or I will be in it? God deals in the right now. The word of God says in Hebrews 11:1, "Now faith is the substance of things hoped for, the evidence of things not seen."

As you desire a closer walk with Him, make up your mind that you are going to allow Him to bless you in this day; heal you in this day; love you in this day.

The Lord's Prayer, which is awesome and very powerful, if we'll pay attention to the words and not treat it like a recital, says in "Matthew 6:6-15:

6 But thou, when thou prayest, enter into thy closet, and when thou hast shut thy door, pray to thy Father which is in secret; and thy Father which seeth in secret shall reward thee openly.

7 But when ye pray, use not vain repetitions, as the

heathen do: for they think that they shall be heard for their much speaking.

8 Be not ye therefore like unto them: for your Father knoweth what things ye have need of, before ye ask him.

9 After this manner therefore pray ye: Our Father which art in heaven, Hallowed be thy name.

10 Thy kingdom come. Thy will be done in earth, as it is in heaven.

11 Give us this day our daily bread.

12 And forgive us our debts, as we forgive our debtors.

13 And lead us not into temptation, but deliver us from evil: For thine is the kingdom, and the power, and the glory, for ever. Amen.

14 For if ye forgive men their trespasses, your heavenly Father will also forgive you:

15 But if ye forgive not men their trespasses, neither will your Father forgive your trespasses.

Now Jesus taught the disciples this prayer, which is still sufficient for us today:

11 Give us this day our daily bread.

12 And forgive us our debts, as we forgive our debtors.

13 And lead us not into temptation, but deliver us from evil: For thine is the kingdom, and the power, and the glory, for ever. Amen."

He was never wrong or out of line. He knew that the day at hand was sufficient unto itself. Not tomorrow, because soon enough, tomorrow would become today.

Many of us have past relationships, past hurts, past bosses, and past lives, that we need to let go….say goodbye to each of them as they are part of yesterday.

Listen, I know that some things are harder than others to let go, but that's where the grace of God comes into play in our lives. As I have previously told you, I think that my name should have been Grace. I sincerely thank God for His grace, as it has been abundant in my life. We win *every time* we obey the voice of the Holy Spirit of the living God.

As much as I loved and cherished my dear daddy, when the Holy Spirit whispered to me one day to *"Let him go,"* it took the grace of God for me to do it. See, almost two years after Daddy had passed away, I was still grieving, literally crying most days. I would hardly let anyone see me, but in my personal quiet time, I would reminisce about all the wonderful times with Daddy while he lived, and would just throw myself a pity party. I don't think I shared with any of my siblings how I would cry almost every night for a year or longer. Now, it was up to me to listen to the Holy

Spirit and let him (Daddy) go, or I could have kept on grieving and crying until now. God wanted me free! See, Daddy *was* free! Hallelujah!

God's grace is so sufficient for **any** situation that we face. Psalm 116:15 reminded me that, "Precious in the sight of the LORD is the death of his saints." That brings me to something else that's wonderful about grace. For it is by grace alone, that we are saved. Not how many times we've gone to church; what year we got saved; how many times we've been baptized; the name of our church or the denomination. Dear sister or brother, it is by God's awesome grace that we are saved. Ephesians 2:8-9 explains this, "For by grace are ye saved through faith; and that not of yourselves: it is the gift of God: Not of works, lest any man should boast."

If the Lord could just get us to believe and receive His "so great a salvation" that we cannot ever earn! If we could just know how much He loves us, just the way we are! Grace is about His love for us, not our love for Him. There are many scriptures in the Bible on Grace and we need to be familiar with them. Too often we forget that it's God's grace that carries us from day to day and lifts us up out of the muck and the mire, the mess and the junk that we sometimes get ourselves into. God's grace is sufficient for anything that we face. We just have to believe it!

So God, Why Am I This Color?

Can anyone tell me what's color got to do with it? Some are asking, "Why wasn't I born with white skin? Why was I born with black skin? Why can't I tan or even be in the sun for extended periods of time?" They may be even shouting at God, "I don't like my color nor its complexities. Why did you make me and my life this way?" The truth of the matter is - your color and its complicated nature will not be changing anytime soon! Sorry!

I often think of five (5) babies lying side by side, very comfortably taking an afternoon nap. They are peacefully sleeping, having been well fed, burped, and placed in a fresh, dry diaper with a little baby powder. A nurse in a maternity ward is working her shift at 3:00 am and notices that there are five (5) new babies lying in their separate incubators. Peering down at them for the first time since they were released into this world, she notices something. Though unspoken, this is what she sees: Five lovely *children* who are all sleeping peacefully; none of them are cooing "move this baby next to me because he is white, brown or red, and does not look like me"; they haven't a care in the world; and they are totally dependent on some adult to meet their every need. These babies have no clue that they even have skin, not to mention the color of it or how much pigmentation they each have. They are totally at peace with themselves and each other. The nurse, who happened to be a Christian, whispered a short prayer. "Lord, let these precious children grow up in love; love for you and for each other. Let them know the peace of God and live to maintain it in the earth all their lives. May their lives glorify you as they obey your commandment to love their neighbor as themselves. In Jesus' name, Amen". She had tears in her eyes as she thought of the awful injustices in the world *just because of skin color*. She had personally experienced mistreatment because of her beautiful, God-given brown skin. She did overcome because she knew and had a relationship with her God and King, Jesus. It made all the difference in her life as she dealt with her daily work.

Let's take a look at the lives of some everyday people who may have wondered, "God, why did you make me this color?" Is it possible that they questioned Him about other physical features? They were asked various questions including: What is your *race?* Where did you grow up? At what age were you aware of your skin color and how? Have you ever questioned God about your color? Should God have made everyone the same?

Charmaine is from San Antonio, Texas and is a sharp,

well rounded, very well traveled and attractive lady who grew up in the state of New York but has lived in many places. She is black or African American, but believes that we are all just members of the *human race.* She was six years old when made aware of her skin color. While riding on a school bus, she was told to "get to the back of the bus" by the bus driver. She didn't mind because as a child, she thought of the back of the bus as more fun because you bounced higher off the ground when the driver hit a bump. She shared this incident with her mother who became sad, but assured Charmaine that *she* had not done anything wrong.

Charmaine stated that she has never wished that she was a different color, but would love to have been slimmer with long hair.

Celia is an old friend from Michigan, born and raised. She is Irish Catholic and has always had respect for all people – this she said was so much easier to do than what her parents had previously taught her. While in college at Michigan State University, she fell in love with a black man. She stated that she had loved him with all of her heart. He wanted to marry her after college, but her father forbid this from happening. At that moment and time in her life, she wanted to be black, and then it wouldn't have mattered, she thought. She continues to have a love and respect for all of

God's created men and women, and has forgiven her father.

Jim is from Queens, New York and has served in the United States military. His family is from Bogota, Colombia in South America. Hispanic, tall, dark and handsome, he has had challenges of his own related to race. He likes everyone, but feels that some people choose to hurt you because you may not look like them. He was age fourteen when others let him know that he was *different*. Another child was very mean to him because of his reddish brown skin tone. Along the way, because of mistreatment, Jim thought that maybe if he had been born with white skin he would not have encountered these problems. He does love who he is and doesn't believe that God should apologize for making different and beautiful people who may not all look alike.

I think of our God as the awesome creative Creator. Just as beautiful flowers, trees, mountains, and even the waters of the earth are different, God *decided* to make mankind with different looks. God does not have to explain why He made different people with various ethnic features – that's what makes Him God – His sovereignty. It is our job to love and treat people, whether they look like us or not, with respect, kindness and love.

The next time that you wonder, "Why am I this color?", make sure you're on your knees when you ask. I believe that you will receive a very simple answer from the Lord: You are fearfully and wonderfully made, and who you are and what you look like, was His decision.

Love and live just as God made you. Choose to be kind to everyone and you will please God and not man. It is our job to love and not to judge. There is but one righteous judge and that is the Lord.

Don't Live Out the Blame Game!

Do you have friends that you don't spend much time with anymore because everything that happens to them is someone else's fault? Sometimes we complain about another being at fault for our woes. Some have heard their grandparents, parents, or siblings blame somebody for their poverty, lack, or bad situation.

There are ethnic groups who blame other ethnic groups for all of the crime in the world. Another ethnic group may blame a different group for all of the hatred and racism in the world. Yet, another group will blame a different group for taking over this land and that land. With all of this bickering and blaming, we get into spoken and unspoken clashes and make needless and unfounded judgements towards one another.

Quite simply put, we have forgotten about the truth of God's Word when it comes to loving our neighbor. We have become so selfish and self-centered, until the problem, whatever it may be, is never "us" and the condition of our hearts, but "them" - it is *their fault*. It's never "me" who could have been nicer, less assuming and judgmental, but "him and his kind." God sees and hears all, and often, He is kicked out of our churches – yes, I said churches, along with homes, schools, and social clubs. We have decided that He doesn't belong in any of them because He and His word go against the norm, or go against my will and what I really want to do.

Many of us would rather blame than apologize. An apology takes your will or your "want to", and then you just do it, get it over with, move on and be free! Too many of us want to hold onto what somebody did to us, rather than to allow God's love to penetrate our hearts to love our brothers and sisters. We all make mistakes, misjudgements, and make bad choices of words at times. However, because of Jesus, no one is beyond redemption and another chance.

Jesus did warn that in the last days there would be offences and offences, to which He said in Matthew 18:7, "Woe unto the world because of **offences**! for it must needs be that offences come; but woe to that man by whom the offence cometh!"

Be quick to forgive your sister or brother and live to be easily forgiven by them. We will have a much better world is we would allow love to be shed abroad in our hearts daily and flow out to others. Sometimes I wonder what the world would be like if God was to supernaturally blindfold each of us and we couldn't judge another by height, weight, hair type, skin color, or any other method of division used to hate or offend.

There are so many of you who God is just waiting to release your business ideas and witty inventions. He is still waiting on you to stop blaming that man or that woman and seek His face. God is time. He has told us that there is a time and a season for everything. He is not going by our clock or calendar. Many of my friends and sometimes my family accuse me of being hard to get in touch with via phone. There are times when it may be difficult for someone to get in touch with me for various reasons. I have learned in this life that some people will talk with you for hours about their wish list, never achieving a thing on the list *because somebody else is preventing them!* Oh really? Others can prevent you only if you allow them. I know a place…a place of peace, perfection, rest, worship, praise, and victory! No man can stop the plan of God. Get off the blame train, get in the presence of God, and get what's yours! Get away….run from blamers and complainers. They will be doing the same thing a year from now. And if that's you….STOP IT!

If someone is oppressive at home or at work, change the battleground…pray. If someone is mean and evil to you for no reason…pray. One lesson that my daddy reiterated often to my siblings and me, was to treat people right. He would say that they may not treat us right, but don't let their faults be your faults. *You* do what is right. He knew that God would see and reward, and He will do just that for you. Don't blame, change your game and win!

His Truth Is Marching

Jesus said that in the last days, nations will rise up against nations and there would be wars and rumors of wars. As the nations rage, there is fighting, killing, genocide, and one army marching against another. As powerful as the United States Navy, Air Force, and Marines are, it is the Army's primary duty to march.

So it is with the Lord's army of believers. We march in the army of the Lord, fully armored with the Word of the Lord which is our sword. God has never lost one battle and has never been defeated. You have to know and believe that you are in the right army. We are overcomers, and we do overcome by the blood of the Lamb and by the word of our testimony. We can march on the front lines of the Lord's army with utmost confidence of who we are and the victory that is ours – it is already won.

God's truth will *always* march *right on*. Many great men, well-educated men, have tried to stop the truth from marching on but unsuccessfully, of course. How in the world can a man stop God Almighty? He simply can't!

He can come up with this movement or that movement, that false religion, this unholy song, or that unholy movie, the Big Bang Theory, scientology, numerology, lie after lie, after lie, but he can never stop God's truth…His Word…Jesus… from marching on.

Why must the truth march? Because it's going somewhere! Read the Bible, and you'll know where it is going. You will not have to guess or believe what anyone else has to say. You'll know without a shadow of a doubt where it's going. In short, the truth is going back to its author…God Himself. Make a decision today to get in step with the truth. You don't have years and years to make a decision. Jesus may not return today, but your appointment to leave this world could be any day. Either way, I wouldn't miss the march. I wouldn't miss the blessed assurance of being with my Savior and marching right on back to the One who created me.

Many are marching to the drum beat of this world and getting rich doing it, I might add. Some have made millions, even billions with their music, performances, New Age meetings and lectures, prostitution, pornography, sports, and the list goes on and on. Jesus said that Satan is the prince of this world. See, Satan will never be king of anything, he's just a prince of a dying world. If you're in his marching band, GET OUT in a hurry! The Bible says in James 4:7, "Submit yourselves therefore to God. Resist the devil, and he will flee from you."

The mere fact is that we are living in the last days. Don't believe it because I am writing it, but believe it because Jesus said this truth in Acts 2:17,

"And it shall come to pass in the last days, saith God, I will pour out My Spirit upon all flesh; and your sons and your daughters shall prophesy, and your young men shall see visions, and your old men shall dream dreams."

If you have ever wanted someone to tell you the truth, I am that someone. God gave me this assignment, and I've written it as He has given it to me. Now that you've heard it, please don't refuse it. God loves you SO MUCH and longs for you to just simply love Him back.

He wants you to come to know Him in His love, in His power, in His joy, in His peace, and in all of His truth. He has waited patiently for you, but Beloved, He says NOW is the hour and the time. With outstretched loving arms, He says, "Come." He's your daddy! The world has a popular saying, "Whose your daddy?" Without a doubt, Father God is your daddy and mine. He has an unconditional love for you. It doesn't matter what you may have done, how you have lived in the past, it's the *right now* that matters most to God.

We Hold These Truths

Although I have had a wonderful life thus far, I like the simple life. By worldly standards, I have been abundantly blessed with fine houses, cars and amazing furnishings. I am a graduate of a renowned college in our nation's capitol and have had illustrious careers. I am an entrepreneur and CEO of my own small companies. Have played semi-pro tennis and on occasion with professional tennis players. I have traveled globally for leisure and evangelism, and having spoken the Word of God in places that I never dreamed possible. I was born into a very large family of love and with many who helped to shape my life. You name it and mostly, I've been blessed to have it or to have had it.

But you know what? With all of my heart I can say that, "I wouldn't trade the truth of the Gospel of Jesus Christ for any of it!" To know Christ is to know Truth. I can say like the Apostle Paul does in Philippians 1:21, "For to me to live is Christ, and to die is gain."

Beloved, God has so much more than - money, houses, cars, land, men, women, or whatever we passionately seek. God knows that we live on earth and are in this world, but not of this world. He does not require us to want to die every day so that we can be with Him. He has need of us on this earth until our time is fulfilled, or He returns and scoops us up in the rapture! If we would make up our minds to serve Him with all of our hearts, souls, minds, and bodies, and then get to work for the kingdom, I believe that He would meet our every need. I didn't say every want, but every need. When we are able to forget about ourselves, concentrate on the goodness of God and the needs of others, I believe that we will see signs, wonders, and so many miracles.

Don't put off receiving Him because you are young or because life has you at this place or that place right now. Remember that "today is the day of salvation."

I polled several young people in particular and asked them to name just two of the Ten Commandments. I also asked them which Biblical character did God use to give them. Most could not do it and thought that Abraham was used by God to give the Ten Commandments. God used Moses to give the Ten Commandments.

What many people don't know and some preachers don't teach is what happened in Exodus 20:18-22 when God spoke these VERY IMPORTANT Commandments, which really are gifts of life from

God. Without them, we would be so lawless and in a world of trouble.

During this time period, Moses would bring the people out of the camp to meet with God. How intimate! Mount Sinai would smoke because the Lord descended upon it in fire, and the whole mountain would quake. Wow! Now, after the Ten Commandments were spoken by God himself, we are told that:

"And all the people saw the thundering, and the lightnings, and the noise of the trumpet, and the mountain smoking: and when the people saw it, they removed, and stood afar off. And they said unto Moses, Speak thou with us, and we will hear: but let not God speak with us, lest we die. And Moses said unto the people, Fear not: for God is come to prove you, and that his fear may be before your faces, that ye sin not. And the people stood afar off, and Moses drew near unto the thick darkness where God was. And the Lord said unto Moses, Thus thou shalt say unto the children of Israel, ye have seen that I have talked with you from heaven."

I find that the Ten Commandments are so plain, easy to read and understand. Take a look at them below. Read them with the intent to obey God for the best life ever. One thing is for sure, we are going to hold some teaching, some ideology, whether true or false, as our truth. Let it be God's Holy Word.

The Ten Commandments Exodus 20:1-17 (With Commentary):

1) Thou shalt have no other gods before me. Thou shalt not bow down thyself to any, nor serve them: for I the Lord thy God am a jealous God.

2) Thou shalt not make unto thee any graven image, or any likeness of any thing that is in heaven above or that is in the earth beneath, or that is in the water under the earth.

3) Thou shalt not take the name of the Lord thy God in vain; for the Lord will not hold him guiltless that take his name in vain.

4) Remember the Sabbath day, to keep it holy. Labor for 6 days, and do all your work. But the seventh day is the Sabbath of the Lord thy God: in it thou shalt not do any work, thou, nor your son, nor your daughter, your manservant, nor your maidservant, nor your cattle, nor your stranger that's within your gates. In 6 days the Lord made heaven and earth, the sea, and all that is in them, and rested the seventh day: wherefore the Lord blessed the Sabbath day, and hallowed it. (He made it HOLY!)

5) Honor thy father and your mother: that your days may be long upon the land which the Lord thy God giveth thee.

6) Thou shalt not kill (Many in the Bible have killed–Moses to name one. He killed an Egyptian to defend a Hebrew brother; David had Uriah, a married woman's husband killed so he could be with her; killing is not pleasing to God.)

7) Thou shalt not commit adultery

   (As mentioned, David committed adultery.... say what? Yes, we are talking about King David, and God Almighty called him "a man after his own heart?" Yes, He did. God alone knows all about you and the substance, the very essence of you. He knows the true woman or man that you are, despite any or all of your shortcomings. God hangs in there with us, so we need to always hang in there with Him – no matter what. Don't EVER allow the devil to tell you it's too late or that "you've really blown it this time." God is the lover of your soul, and His love is everlasting. One of the primary things about adultery is that God doesn't want us to split our affections. Once we've made a commitment - a covenant with someone – both parties are to keep it.

   It's like making a commitment and a covenant with God. That's why marriage is to be taken seriously...it's a commitment and a covenant between God and a man and a woman. Make sure that the person that you marry loves God as much or more than you do. If not, it may be a disaster from the beginning. I am just telling the truth!")

15) Thou shalt not steal.

16) Thou shalt not bear false witness against thy neighbour.

17) Thou shalt not covet thy neighbour's house, thou shalt not covet thy neighbour's wife, nor his manservant, nor his maidservant, nor his ox, nor his ass, nor any thing that is thy neighbour's.

Many of the establishments in America, including government buildings and schools, used to have these commandments written on the walls or framed and placed on the wall, but much of it has now been removed. When we get God's Word into our hearts, it doesn't matter what man takes away in the natural.

God has written his everlasting word upon our hearts that we might not sin against Him.

Let each of us purpose in our hearts to know the Truth and allow it to make us free, everyday! God's Word is Truth, and will never, ever change.

Prayer For Salvation

Dear God, in the name of your Son, Jesus Christ, here I am. In your Word you said that whosoever shall call upon the name of the Lord shall be saved (Romans 10:13). Right now, I am calling upon the name of Jesus because I know and believe that He died on the cross at Calvary just for me – to remove my sins. He was indeed raised from the dead on the third day.

I am asking you now Lord Jesus, to come into my heart, forgive all of my sins, deliver me from my past, and heal all of my diseases. I choose to live to please you in every way, every day. I fully yield myself to you now, and I know that I am a new creation. Thank you Jesus – you are my Lord and Savior!

In Jesus' name, Amen.

We will continue to pray for you and your relationship with the Lord Jesus.

About the Author

Gaynell Jones Montgomery is the eighth child of fifteen, born to Julia Jones and the late Elbert Jones of Greenville, MS. She is proud to have spent her first seven formative years of school in the San Antonio, TX school system due to her Army Veteran dad's Civil Service employment. She completed high school in the MS Delta at Greenville High school where she was a cheerleader, student council member, Home Court Maid, tennis player, and member of several clubs. Gaynell received her BBA degree from Howard University in Washington, DC. She enjoys many hobbies but ministering God's Word through various methods, playing tennis, and global travel are her favorites. She is an Author, Trainer, Producer, Playwright, and Tennis Clinic Instructor.

Today, Gaynell is an Independent Career Manager in the Insurance Industry. She is CEO of her enterprise, Majestic Travel based in Memphis, TX and managed by Sylvia Hardy. Also, she is developing several other enterprises such as Majestic Moments, which comprises a host of products like pillows, pillowcases, tote bags, etcetera. Her businesses were birthed out of her love for people to experience God's beautiful world as she has and her product line carries the Word of God to remind others that God is the Source of it all!

FOR MORE INFORMATION

Please contact us at:

Gaynell Montgomery/Majestic Moments

835 East Lamar Blvd, #446

Arlington, TX 76011

(972)697-7072

Email: majestimoments@gmail.com

CPSIA information can be obtained
at www.ICGtesting.com
Printed in the USA
FFOW05n0138250217